LANCASTER
COUNTY

Out &
About

photography by

Patti Thompson

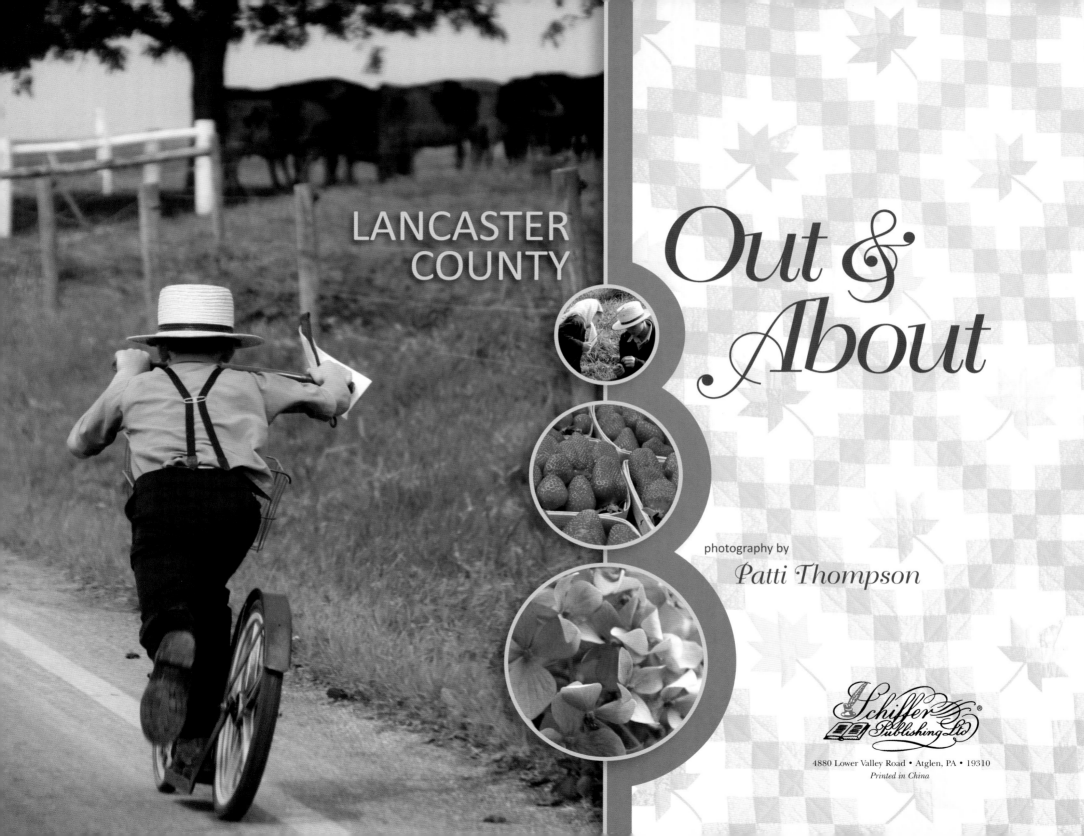

LANCASTER COUNTY

Out & About

photography by
Patti Thompson

Schiffer
Publishing Ltd®

4880 Lower Valley Road • Atglen, PA • 19310
Printed in China

Faces of Lancaster County, 978-0-7643-3707-9, $29.99

Lancaster County Reflections, 978-0-7643-3584-6, $24.99

Bridges of Lancaster County, 978-0-7643-3427-6, $24.99

Designed by Danielle D. Farmer
Cover Design by Bruce M. Waters
Type set in Bellevue/Calibri

ISBN: 978-0-7643-3923-3
Printed in China

Schiffer Books are available at special discounts for bulk purchases for sales promotions or premiums. Special editions, including personalized covers, corporate imprints, and excerpts can be created in large quantities for special needs. For more information contact the publisher:

Published by Schiffer Publishing Ltd.
4880 Lower Valley Road
Atglen, PA 19310
Phone: (610) 593-1777; Fax: (610) 593-2002
E-mail: Info@schifferbooks.com

For the largest selection of fine reference books on this and related subjects, please visit our website at
www.schifferbooks.com

We are always looking for people to write books on new and related subjects. If you have an idea for a book, please contact us at
proposals@schifferbooks.com

This book may be purchased from the publisher.
Include $5.00 for shipping.
Please try your bookstore first.
You may write for a free catalog.

In Europe, Schiffer books are distributed by
Bushwood Books
6 Marksbury Ave.
Kew Gardens
Surrey TW9 4JF England
Phone: 44 (0) 20 8392 8585; Fax: 44 (0) 20 8392 9876
E-mail: info@bushwoodbooks.co.uk
Website: www.bushwoodbooks.co.uk

Dedication

To my husband Ken, with all my love, without whom this book would not exist.

To my children Lauren and Ethan, always loved, my constant encouragers.

To my lifelong friend Eve, who first envisioned this book.

Introduction

Lancaster County Out & About will have meaning to you if you have simply driven through on your way to somewhere else and thought, "Oh—we need to stop here!" Or if you fondly remember a leisurely vacation when you enjoyed the sounds of the Amish horses clopping by as you woke in a quaint bed and breakfast. Or if, as Patti Thompson, you have loved the Lancaster countryside and people from your youth. Patti's love for her home is evident in every image. Travel with Patti now to visit Lancaster County, Pennsylvania, and reflect on its beauty and peacefulness.

13

GERMAN
REFORMED
CHURCH
CEMETERY
1755 TO 1861

Home grown STRAWBERRIES $4.50 Box

Fresh Picked Local Raspberries 2.50 ½ pint 5.00 pint

Q's Looms

Fresh Local and Heirloom Products From the Heart of Lancaster County Just like Grandma and her Grandma

Homade Baked w/

Zinnia 4½ pot $2.50 EA 3 for $7.00

Good Harvest
FARM MARKET
& GREENHOUSE

FRESH
STRAWBERRIES
HANGING
BASKETS
BEDDING
PLANTS
READY NOW!

STRAYER-UPTON

PRACTICAL

ARITHMETICS

SECOND BOOK

THREE-BOOK SERIES

WITH

ANSWERS

THE NEW MORE STREETS and ROADS

3²

THE NEW "OUR NEW FRIENDS"

Grade 6

STEP BY STEP

PATHWAY

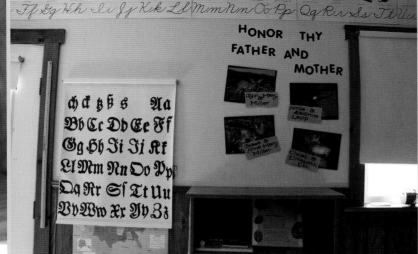

CENTRAL MARKET

FRESH-HOME-MADE
JAMS-AND-JELLYS

HOME MADE
CANNED
GOODES

BAKED GOODS

MAPLE
SYRUP

POTPIE
AND
NOODLE

Sweet
coRn
(Ambrosia)
$ 3.00 @ doz.
1.75 ½ doz.

COUNTRYSIDE ROADSTAND
HOME MADE
BAKEDGOODS
CANNEDGOODS
ROOT BEER
SOFT PRETZELS
ICE CREAM
NOODLES
CANDY CHIPS
QUILTS CRAFTS
¼ MILE →

JESUS SAID!
"COME UNTO ME, ALL YE
THAT LABOR AND ARE
HEAVY LADEN, AND I
WILL GIVE YOU REST."

WAY SIDE GOSPEL CRUSADERS
1647 OLD PHILA PIKE LANCASTER, PA.

MATT. 11:28

SEASONED
CUT TO
FIREPLACE
LENGTH
APPLE

HOMEGROWN
APPLES

Locations Index